INSIDE MARTIAL ARTS

JUDO

柔道　柔道

by Annabelle Tometich

Content Consultant:
Sayaka Torra, 2008 Olympian & 5th Degree Black Belt,
East Bay Judo Institute

SportsZone
An Imprint of Abdo Publishing | www.abdopublishing.com

www.abdopublishing.com

Published by Abdo Publishing, a division of ABDO, PO Box 398166, Minneapolis, Minnesota 55439. Copyright © 2015 by Abdo Consulting Group, Inc. International copyrights reserved in all countries. No part of this book may be reproduced in any form without written permission from the publisher. SportsZone™ is a trademark and logo of Abdo Publishing.

Printed in the United States of America, North Mankato, Minnesota
102014
012015

THIS BOOK CONTAINS
RECYCLED MATERIALS

Cover Photo: Tibor Illyes/AP Images
Interior Photos: Tibor Illyes/AP Images, 1; Wu Xiaoling/Xinhua Press/Corbis, 4–5; Paul Sancya/AP Images, 6; David Cumming/Eye Ubiquitous/Alamy, 9; AP Images, 10–11, 43; Shamil Zhumatov/Reuters/Newscom, 12; Aflo Sport/Glow Images, 13, 22–23, 30–31; Aflo Score/Glow Images, 15; Yuri Arcurs Media/SuperStock, 17; Ben Curtis/AP Images, 18; Enrico Calderoni/Aflo/Newscom, 19, 20 (top), 20 (bottom), 21 (top), 21 (bottom), 25; Andrey Kaderov/iStockphoto, 26; Yutaka/Aflo/Newscom, 28; Facundo Arrizabalaga/EPA/Newscom, 29; Nick Potts/PA Wire/AP Images, 33; Terry Schmitt/UPI/Newscom, 34; Koji Sasahara/AP Images, 36–37; Kazuhiro Nogi/AFP/Getty Images/Newscom, 38; Ng Han Guan/AP Images, 40; Kyodo/AP Images, 44

Editor: Thomas K. Adamson
Series Designer: Becky Daum

Library of Congress Control Number: 2014944200

Cataloging-in-Publication Data
Tometich, Annabelle.
 Judo / Annabelle Tometich.
   p. cm. – (Inside martial arts)
ISBN 978-1-62403-602-6 (lib. bdg.)
Includes bibliographical references and index.
1. Judo–Juvenile literature.   I. Title.
796.815/2–dc23

2014944200

TABLE OF CONTENTS

CHAPTER 1

OLYMPIC WIN

With less than two minutes left in their match, Mansur Isaev of Russia and Riki Nakaya of Japan circled each other on the mat. They were competing for a gold medal in judo at the 2012 summer Olympic Games in London, England. Neither Isaev nor Nakaya had scored a point.

The men locked hands. Nakaya slipped an arm under Isaev's leg and tried to throw him to the ground.

Mansur Isaev of Russia takes down Riki Nakaya of Japan during the gold medal match at the 2012 summer Olympic Games in London, England.

It looked like Isaev was going down. But in the blink of an eye, Isaev wrapped his leg around Nakaya's and brought him down instead.

Nakaya lay face down on the mat, stunned. Isaev's lightning fast reflexes had earned him the only point of the match. The Russian had won an Olympic gold medal.

Judo is a martial art. The sport was created in 1882. Judo does not use weapons. Instead, it combines full body contact with mindfulness for the opponent.

Judo started in Japan. The sport's founder was Dr. Jigoro Kano. As a child, Kano was smaller than most kids his age. He was tired of being bullied. He dreamed of being strong.

Kano became fascinated by the Japanese martial art of jujutsu. In jujutsu, fighters attack and defend themselves using their entire bodies. With jujutsu, small people can defeat stronger people by fighting smartly. Kano wanted to learn everything about the sport.

Isaev shows off his Olympic gold medal in judo.

Kano learned jujutsu quickly. At age 19, he showed his jujutsu skills to the president of the United States.

Kano started to teach jujutsu, but he soon figured out a unique style of fighting. His style used throwing, grappling, and striking.

Kano would dodge his opponents' attacks. He would get them off balance, so it would take less strength to defeat them. Kano called his new martial art "judo."

In 1882, Kano founded the Kodokan dojo in Tokyo, Japan. In Japanese, *dojo* means "a place to learn the way." Dojos are training centers for martial arts.

Kano believed judo could be studied for years without

KANO'S EXAMPLE

On a ship voyaging to Europe in 1889, a man made fun of Jigoro Kano. Kano threw the man down but kept his hand under the man's head so he wouldn't get hurt. In those few seconds, Kano showed how judo combines powerful technique with mindfulness for the opponent.

Judo is popular worldwide for all ages.

being mastered. He saw judo and its focus on gentleness as a way of life.

At the 1932 Olympic Games in Los Angeles, California, Kano introduced judo to the world. About 200 of his students demonstrated the new sport. Judo became an Olympic sport in 1964. Tokyo, Japan, hosted the Olympics that year.

Kano died in 1938, but judo lived on. More than 20 million people in the world practice judo. It's all thanks to Jigoro Kano, a boy tired of being bullied.

CHAPTER 2

TECHNIQUES AND MOVES

People who practice judo are called judokas. A judoka's uniform is called a *judogi*. It is called a *gi* for short. Kano created the gi based on traditional Japanese clothing. Gis are white to represent purity and simplicity. A gi has three parts. The jacket is called a *uwagi*. The cotton pants are called *shitabaki*. The belt is called an *obi*.

A white gi represents purity and simplicity.

Bowing during judo practice is a sign of respect.

Gis must fit properly. Shitabaki should reach the ankles. The uwagi's sleeves should reach the fists when the arms are at the side. The uwagi is usually made of heavy cloth. Thick cloth is harder for an opponent to grab.

A gi that does not fit can create an advantage. If it is too tight, the opponent won't be able to grasp it. If it is too loose, it may be too easy to grasp. If a judoka's gi does not

meet required measurements, he or she cannot compete.

In judo, competitions are used to test a judoka's skills.

In matches, judokas score points by throwing and pinning

The judo stance called *shizen-tai* allows a judoka to be ready for attack at any time.

their opponent for certain lengths of time. Before competing, beginners must learn the basics.

Every beginner judoka must learn a standing bow. This is called a *ritsu-rei*. Judokas stand with their arms at their sides. They bend at the waist. They keep their back straight. The ritsu-rei is a sign of respect. Judokas bow before and after practices. They also bow to their partners during practice and to their opponents before and after competition.

After a bow, judokas stand in *shizen-tai*. This is the combat stance. Judokas stand with their feet shoulder-width apart. They keep their backs straight. Their arms rest at their sides. Shizen-tai creates stability. It allows a judoka to attack at any moment. Shizen-tai is more than just a stance, though. It is a state of mind. Judokas should always be on the attack, no matter their position. Even if a judoka has been thrown to the ground, he or she should be

Getting an opponent off balance is key to a good throw in judo.

thinking about how to return the attack. This is the attitude of shizen–tai.

Judo has three types of techniques. There is throwing, grappling, and striking. Striking is only used in a type of training called *kata*. These techniques are called *waza*. Waza are used to score points. Good waza can also make opponents submit or quit the match.

Throwing techniques are known as *nage-waza*. They involve lifting opponents or shifting them off balance. Opponents are then thrown to the ground. The person doing the throw is usually standing. Sometimes judokas will put themselves on the ground to do a throw. This puts them in an unfavorable position. These are called sacrifice throws.

Grappling techniques are used when both opponents are on the ground. They are known as *katame-waza*. The three types of grappling techniques are pinning, choking, and joint locking. For pinning, judokas hold their opponent's

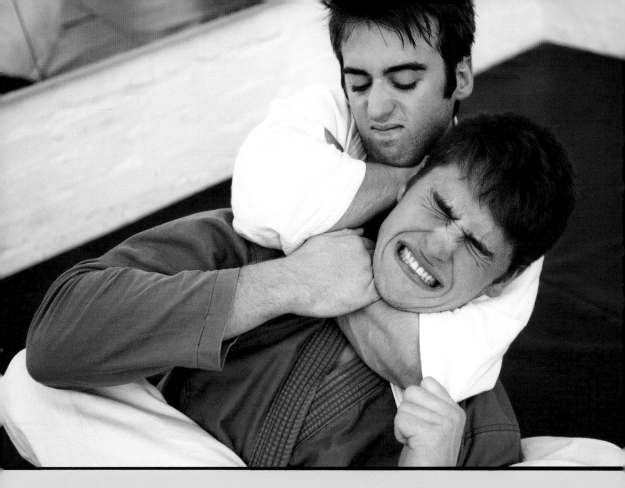

Choking can force an opponent to submit.

back against the ground. A judoka can win by pinning the opponent to the ground for several seconds.

Chokes prevent an opponent from breathing. Chokes force an opponent to submit or risk passing out. In arm locking, judokas put pressure on their opponent's elbow. Judokas can grasp their opponent's elbow with their

**An arm lock is a great way to make a
judo opponent unable to move.**

arms, legs, or knees. They then bend the elbow backward

to lock it. Choking and arm locking are allowed only for

advanced judokas.

Striking techniques are called *atemi-waza*. Judokas strike with their arms and legs. Strikes are not used in competition. Strikes are meant to be studied. They are only used in training.

Judokas can practice for a lifetime trying to master skills. Judo has hundreds of techniques. There are 67 different kinds of throws alone.

Striking techniques in judo are used only in training or for demonstrations.

JUDO THROW

Judokas can use their opponent's own weight against them in a throw.

Getting the opponent off balance is the key to a successful throw.

A throw with more force and speed scores higher in competition.

The throw is completed when the opponent is on the ground.

CHAPTER 3
TRAINING

You can tell how experienced judokas are by the color of their belts. The most experienced judo athletes wear black belts. People just starting judo wear white belts around their gis.

Belts were not always a part of judo. Dojos once awarded certificates or scrolls. The scrolls recognized achievement. Achievement is now measured through ranks called *kyu*.

The most experienced judokas wear black belts.

There are six kyu ranks. Further rankings are called *dans*. These are the expert ranks. The highest dan ranking ever earned was the 10th dan.

Belt colors vary by country. They also vary among the different judo organizations. However, a judoka's first belt is always white. The black belt is always the highest.

A white belt shows a judoka who is empty. As judo athletes learn, they fill with knowledge. They earn darker belts. These typically include yellow, orange, green, blue, purple, brown, and then black. A black belt does not always signify a great fighter. The belt represents knowledge and skill.

THE FIRST 10TH DAN

Only 16 judokas have ever earned the 10th dan. That is the highest degree of black belt ever awarded by the Kodokan ranking system. Yoshitsugu Yamashita was the first judoka to be promoted to the 10th dan. He helped found the Kodokan. Yamashita traveled to the United States. He taught judo to President Theodore Roosevelt. Yamashita was honored with the 10th dan after his death in 1935.

Kata training can even use fake weapons to show how judo can be used in self-defense.

To advance to a new rank, judokas must meet certain requirements. These requirements can vary by a dojo's teacher, called a *sensei*. Requirements also vary by the organization a dojo follows. It takes years of training to become a black belt.

Gemma Howell, *right*, works on throws with Sensei
Go Tsunoda during a training session.

Judo's three training methods are *kata*, *randori*, and
shiai. The word *kata* means "forms." Kata are planned
patterns of techniques. Judokas practice kata with a partner.
Each opponent knows what will happen next. Judoka use
kata to master new and different methods.

Randori means "free practice." Randori can be very simple and slow. It can also be intense, like competition judo.

Shiai are judo matches. Judokas test their skills in competitions. Judokas also test their strengths and learn their weaknesses through competition.

Beginning judokas train with other judokas who are much better than they are. The beginners get thrown around a lot. They learn how to fall. Falling is a basic skill in judo. Beginners also learn how to protect themselves and how to keep trying even after being thrown.

After learning these basics, judokas of the same level train together. This training mimics judo matches. Judokas then train against opponents who are not as good as they are. This teaches the judoka the correct body movements. Judokas learn how to throw opponents. They learn how to use their techniques properly.

**Judokas who have earned a black belt train
hard to continue to master their skills.**

Judo practice is not about winning matches. Judo practice is about improving skills. It is also about getting better at techniques and improving as a person.

Expert judokas believe fighters should train long and hard before competing in matches. The way a judoka wins a match is as important as the winning itself. Experts believe judokas must face their opponents. They must try to stay ahead of them. They must not run away or quit if things get difficult.

That is how Kazuzo Kudo trained his judokas. Kudo was a ninth-dan black belt. He practiced under Jigoro Kano. Kudo believed judokas should fight to the very end. He taught

them to never quit and to always look for their chance to

break through. Kudo believed a good attitude made victory

much sweeter.

**Judokas train for a long time before
they are ready for competition.**

CHAPTER 4
ADVANCED JUDO

In Japan, the first black belt level is *shodan*. *Shodan* means "first level" or "beginning step." In judo, the black belt is not the end. It marks the beginning of a new stage of training.

Judokas must practice for years to earn a black belt. From there, it can take decades or even a lifetime to earn the highest dans.

Even judokas with a black belt continue training and practicing throws.

DAN LEVELS

Each of the 10 black belt *dans*, or stages, has a name. The 10 dans are *shodan, nidan, sandan, yodan, godan, rokudan, shichidan, hachidan, kudan*, and *judan*. Judan, the 10th level, takes its name from judo. *Judan* means "gentle stage."

There is no formula for earning a black belt. Many sensei believe judokas should not train just for belts. Training should be done for improvement. To earn a black belt, a judoka must show mastery of many skills.

These skills go beyond throws and grips. They include conduct and character. They also include maturity. Black belts must know judo's history. They must follow judo's principles of gentleness. Black belts understand how the ideas learned in judo can apply to other parts of their lives. They are constantly striving to be better.

Black belts show mastery in several throws. They have mastered using their hands, hips, and feet for throws. They

In competition, judokas show that they have mastered techniques such as throws. Kayla Harrison, *right*, is an example of how training pays off.

have also perfected sacrifice throws. In addition, a black belt knows how to escape from holds and chokes.

Kayla Harrison is a great example of what it takes to succeed in judo. She became the first US Olympian to win a gold medal for judo. She won it at the 2012 Olympics in London, England. Harrison started judo at age six. To train, she ran and lifted weights. She sparred with partners. She soon became the best at her sport. Yet she still spent

Kayla Harrison waves from the medal podium after winning gold at the 2012 Olympic Games.

two hours each day practicing throws and holds. Harrison practiced judo techniques over and over. She understood that a technique could not be mastered. Techniques must be constantly used to better understand them.

The highest black belt dans have no formal requirements. Judokas who earn ninth-degree black belts are called kudan. Judan are 10th-degree black belts. Kudan and judan are known for being excellent teachers. They spread the ideas of judo throughout the world.

These elite judokas make judo their lives. In 2011, Keiko Fukuda became the first woman to earn the 10th dan of black belt. She had to give up a lot to earn this honor. She left her family in Japan. Fukuda traveled the world studying and teaching. She devoted her life to judo.

The Kodokan has never awarded an 11th-dan black belt. An 11th-dan black belt is possible, though. Kano said judo should have no limit. He said if a judoka reaches a level beyond judan, then an 11th dan should be awarded.

It would take an exceptional judoka to earn an 11th dan. There are about 20 million judokas in the world. The first 11th dan could be one of them. With judo, the possibilities are limitless.

CHAPTER 5

COMPETITIONS

Judokas train long and hard to learn techniques. They then test their skills in competitions. Judo matches are called shiai.

It can take many months before a sensei thinks a student is ready for shiai. In competition, judokas face similar opponents. Competitors are usually the same size, age, and skill level.

Once they are ready for competition, judokas have to be ready to fight hard for wins.

Win or lose, judokas bow at the end of a match.

In shiai, one judoka wears all white. The other judoka

wears a blue belt or a blue gi. Opponents bow before

entering the competition area. They bow again before

stepping onto the mat. They bow a third time to each other before starting the match. These bows show respect for the competition and the opponent.

A match starts when the referee says *"hajime." Hajime* is Japanese for "begin." When the referee says *"matte,"* the match is paused. *Matte* means "wait" in Japanese. Matte is called when a contestant needs to adjust his or her uniform. Matte is also called for injuries. It's also called when the judokas are not attempting enough waza. A judoka cannot stall. Opponents must always try to make a move.

There are three types of offensive scores in shiai. They are *ippon*, *wazari*, and *yuko*.

An ippon ends the match. An ippon is like a pin in wrestling or a knockout in boxing. Ippon is scored when a judoka throws his or her opponent. To be an ippon, the throw must have great force and great speed. The throw must also put the opponent on his or her back. The referee decides if the throw has all three elements.

The referee says when points are scored during the match.

An ippon can also be scored by holding or pinning an opponent for 25 seconds. In addition, it can be scored when an opponent submits by tapping with their hand or foot. The judoka can also tell the referee that he or she submits. Such tap outs often result from chokes or arm locks.

A wazari is scored when a judoka's throw does not show enough control to be an ippon. Wazari is awarded for pins that last longer than 20 seconds but not more than 25 seconds. Two wazaris equal one ippon. After two wazaris, the match ends.

Yuko is scored for throws that lack two or more ippon elements. Yuko is also awarded for pins lasting 15 to 19 seconds.

Judges track the scores. If neither judoka scores an ippon, then the contestant with the most wazaris and yukos wins. But a wazari wins over any number of yukos.

Shidos are minor judo penalties. Major penalties are *hansoku-make*. A contestant who receives a hansoku-make is disqualified from the match. Their opponent is awarded ippon. Hansoku-make is called when a judoka ignores the referee's instructions or when a judoka intentionally tries to endanger the opponent. If a player has a certain number of shidos and then scores a yuko or wazari, they win.

Penalties can only win the match if there are no offensive scores. If neither judoka has scored any wazaris or yukos, the judoka with fewer shidos wins.

If the score is tied at the end of a match, it goes to a Golden Score period. In Golden Score, the first judoka to score wins. If one player gets a penalty, the other player wins. There is no time limit. Overtime continues until there is a winner.

A judoka's first competition is usually local. As contestants improve, they can advance to bigger shiai. The highest levels of competition take place at the World Judo Championships (WJC) and the Olympic Games. The WJC are held once a year. However, every fourth year they are not held. The Olympics serve as the championship for those years.

The WJC are held by the International Judo Federation (IJF). The IJF is one of the major governing bodies for judo.

Judo became an Olympic sport for the 1964 Games in Tokyo, Japan. Isao Inokuma of Japan, *right*, won a gold medal.

The WJC started in 1954. Back then, it was just for men. The WJC added a women's division in 1980.

Judo made its Olympic debut at the 1964 Olympic Games in Tokyo, Japan. There were 74 judokas from 27 countries. At the 2012 Olympics in London, England,

Wojdan Shahrkani, *right*, was allowed to wear a head covering while she competed in the 2012 Olympics in London, England.

387 judo athletes competed. They represented 135 countries. Women judokas did not compete for Olympic medals until 1992.

The world's best judokas have also competed in other sports. They have gone on to succeed in wrestling and mixed martial arts.

Judo requires speed, strength, and intelligence. Yet it focuses on gentleness and care for opponents. The popularity of this serious martial art continues to increase around the world.

WOJDAN SHAHRKANI

At the 2012 Olympics, judoka Wojdan Shahrkani made history. Shahrkani became the first woman from Saudi Arabia to compete at the Olympic Games. Saudi Arabia has strict rules for women. Saudi Arabian women must wear long black dresses, called abaya, when in public. They must also wear head and face scarves. This makes it tough for Saudi Arabian women to train in sports. Shahrkani was only 16 years old when she competed in the Olympics. She became famous all over the world. She lost in her opening match. Yet she called the experience "the opportunity of a lifetime."

GLOSSARY

formula
A plan or method for doing something.

grappling
The act of gripping or seizing someone or something, as in wrestling.

kata
Planned patterns of judo techniques used in training; each opponent knows what will happen next.

knockout
A punch or blow that leaves an opponent unable to compete further.

maturity
The state of being fully developed.

mixed martial arts
A combat sport that combines elements of wrestling, boxing, judo, and other martial arts.

pinning
To hold an opponent on his or her back with one or both shoulders against the ground.

referee
A judge who enforces the rules of a sport.

FOR MORE INFORMATION

Further Readings

Martin, Ashley P. *How to Improve at Judo*. New York: Crabtree, 2009.

Ohlenkamp, Neil. *Black Belt: Judo Skills and Techniques*. London, UK: New Holland, 2006.

Watson, Brian. *Judo Memoirs of Jigoro Kano: Early History of Judo*. Victoria, BC: Trafford, 2008.

Websites

To learn more about Inside Martial Arts, visit **booklinks.abdopublishing.com**. These links are routinely monitored and updated to provide the most current information available.

INDEX

ABOUT THE AUTHOR

Annabelle Tometich is an award-winning writer and reporter. She has written several children's books on topics ranging from lacrosse and gymnastics to nutrition and popular culture. Annabelle lives in Fort Myers, Florida, with her husband and their two really cute kids.